T0055959

Gabriel

FAURÉ

CANTIQUE DE JEAN RACINE

Canticle of Jean Racine
Op. 11 (1865)

edited
with English translation
by

JOHN RUTTER

for SATB chorus and organ, or piano,
or lower strings and harp (see p. 2)

VOCAL SCORE

MUSIC DEPARTMENT

OXFORD
UNIVERSITY PRESS

For copyright reasons, this edition is not for sale in
Colombia, Cuba, Belgium, France, Italy, Panama, or Spain.

OXFORD
UNIVERSITY PRESS

Great Clarendon Street, Oxford OX2 6DP, England
198 Madison Avenue, New York, NY10016, USA

Oxford University Press is a department of the University of Oxford
It furthers the University's aim of excellence in research, scholarship,
and education by publishing worldwide

Oxford is a registered trade mark of Oxford University Press
in the UK and certain other countries

Database right Oxford University Press (maker)

© Oxford University Press 1986

All rights reserved. No part of this publication may be reproduced,
stored in a retrieval system, or transmitted, in any form or by any means,
without the prior permission in writing of Oxford University Press,
or as expressly permitted by law. Enquiries concerning reproduction
outside the scope of the above should be sent to the Music Copyright
Department, Oxford University Press, at the address above

Permission to perform the works in this anthology in public
(except in the course of divine worship) should normally be obtained
from the Performing Right Society Ltd. (PRS), 29/33 Berners Street,
London W1T 3AB, or its affiliated Societies in each country throughout
the world, unless the owner or the occupier of the premises
being used holds a licence from the Society

Permission to make a recording must be obtained in advance
from the Mechanical Copyright Protection Society Ltd. (MCPS),
Elgar House, 41 Streatham High Road, London SW16 1ER,
or its affiliated Societies in each country throughout the world

---

This piece has been transcribed by the editor for

violas (minimum 2)
cellos (minimum 2)
basses (minimum 2)
harp

Full scores and instrumental parts are available on hire from the publisher.
An upper voice arrangement (S.S.A.A.) with Fauré's original keyboard accompaniment
is also available (Oxford University Press, ISBN 0 19 342611 0).

This edition of *Cantique de Jean Racine* has been recorded
(together with the Fauré *Requiem*, 1893 version) by the Cambridge Singers
and members of the City of London Sinfonia, conducted by John Rutter, on
Conifer CFRA 122 (cassette MCFRA 122, compact disc CDCFRA 122).

CANTIQUE DE JEAN RACINE

Canticle of Jean Racine

Words by
JEAN RACINE
from *Hymnes traduites du bréviare romain*
tr. John Rutter

GABRIEL FAURÉ
Op. 11 (1865)
edited by John Rutter

© Oxford University Press 1986

Printed in Great Britain

OXFORD UNIVERSITY PRESS, MUSIC DEPARTMENT, GREAT CLARENDON STREET, OXFORD OX2 6DP

Photocopying this copyright material is ILLEGAL.

16
S.
A.
T.
-tre u - ni - que es - pé - - ran - - - - ce, Jour é - - - - ter - - -
hope and con - so - la - - - - tion, E - ter - - - - nal
B.
-tre u - ni - que es - pé - - ran - - - - ce, Jour é - - - - ter - - -
hope and con - so - la - - - - tion, E - ter - - - - nal
19
SOPRANOS pp
Nous
Our
ALTOS pp
De la pai - si - ble nuit nous
The peace - ful night is past; our
-nel de la ter - - - re et des cieux, nous
light of the heav'ns and the earth: our
-nel de la ter - - - re et des cieux, nous
light of the heav'ns and the earth: our

22
rom - pons le si - - len - - ce, Di - vin Sau - -
voi - ces greet the morn - - ing; Look down, O
25
- veur, jet - - te sur nous les yeux,
Lord, and hear thy peo - ple's prayer,
cresc.
- veur, jet - te sur nous les yeux, Di -
Lord, and hear thy peo - - ple's prayer, Look
cresc.
cresc.
B
28
f
diminuendo
p
- vin Sau - - veur, jet - te sur nous les
down, O Lord, and hear thy peo - - ple's
f
diminuendo
p
B
f
dimin.
p

31
yeux!
prayer!
il canto marcato
35
pp
39
dolce
C
Ré - pands sur nous le feu de ta
In - spire us, Lord, we pray, With the
dolce
C

42
cresc.
grâ - - ce puis - san - - te, que tout l'en - -
pow'r of thy Spi - - rit, That hell may
cresc.
[cresc.]
45
f
p subito
- fer, que tout l'en - fer fuie au son de ta voix, Dis -
flee, that hell may flee be - fore thy migh - - ty word. From
f
f
p subito
48
- si - - pe le som - meil d'une â - me lan - guis -
slum - - ber wa - ken us, our wea - ry souls re -
p
Dis - si - pe le som - meil lan - - guis -
From slum - ber wa - ken us, our souls re -

51
D
mf
- san - - te, qui la con -
- vi - - ving, That we may
mf
- san - - te, qui la con -
- vi - - ving, That we may
mf
- san - - te, qui la con - duit à l'ou -
- vi - - ving, That we may ne - - ver for -
mf
- san - - te, qui la con - - duit à l'ou -
- vi - - ving, That we may ne - - ver for -
D
mf
54
- duit à l'ou - bli de tes lois,
ne - ver for - get thy laws!
f
- duit à l'ou - bli de tes lois, qui
ne - ver for - get thy laws! That
f
- bli de tes lois, qui la con -
- get all thy laws! That we may
f
- bli de tes lois, qui la con - -
- get all thy laws ! That we may
f

57
f
E
qui la con - duit à l'ou-bli de tes lois!
That we may ne - ver for-get thy laws!
la con - duit à l'ou-bli de tes lois!
we may ne - ver for-get thy laws!
-duit à l'ou - bli de tes lois!
ne - ver for - get all thy laws!
p
-duit à l'ou - bli de tes lois! Ô Christ, sois fa - vo -
ne - ver for - get all thy laws! Lord Je - sus Christ, have
E
dimin.
p
sempre legato

61
p
à ce peu - ple fi - dè - le pour te bé -
on thy faith - ful con - gre - ga - tion Now ga - thered
-ra - ble à ce peu - ple fi - dè - le pour te bé -
mer - cy on thy con - gre - ga - tion Now ga - thered

65
p
Re -
Re -
p
Re - çois les chants qu'il of - - fre,
Re - ceive the hymns they of - - fer
- nir main - te - nant ras - sem - blé,
here in the sight of thy throne;
- nir main - te - nant ras - sem - blé, Re - çois les
here in the sight of thy throne; Re - ceive the
68
cresc.
- çois les chants qu'il of - - fre, à ta gloi - re im - mor - tel - - le, et
- ceive the hymns they of - - fer to thy e - ter - nal glo - - ry; Re -
cresc.
à ta gloi - - re im - - mor - tel - - le, et
to thy glo - - ry, to thy glo - - ry; Re -
cresc.
à ta gloi - - re im - mor - - tel - - le, et
to thy glo - - ry, to thy glo - - ry; Re -
cresc.
chants qu'il of - fre à ta gloi - re im - mor - - tel - - le, et
hymns they of - fer to thy end - - less glo - - ry; Re -
cresc.

72
F
f sempre
de tes dons qu'il re - tour - - ne com-
- newed by thy gifts may they go forth in
F
f sempre
f
75
pp subito
Et de
Re - newed
- blé, Et de tes dons qu'il re -
peace, Re - - newed by thy gifts may they
pp subito
pp subito
78
pp
- tour - - ne com - blé!
go forth in peace.
pp
dolce

Reproduced and printed by
Halstan & Co. Ltd., Amersham, Bucks., England